feel that you are a partner with us. I hope one day to meet you in person. You are doing a great job already. Looking forward to watching your story build and your influence rise!

Sincerely,

FACE VALUE

Building Influence by Giving Value to Others

BRAD ABERNATHY

Edited by Katherine S. Jones

Printed in the United States of America

First Printing, 2019

ISBN: 978-1-54397-832-2

BookBaby Publishing

7905 North Crescent Boulevard

Pennsauken, NJ 08110

www.bookbaby.com

For Jill. You love books. I wrote one for your library.

TABLE OF CONTENTS

1

EXTRAORDINARY THINGS ARE POSSIBLE

Extraordinary things, events, reactions, and relationships are possible. The first sentence of a book -- written by a non-writer -- took a very long time to put into words, but there it is. This sentence is the sole reason I am motivated to write this book. My name is Brad Abernathy. I am the proud wearer of many hats. I am a Christian, a husband to Jill, and a father to Sadie and Kate. I am also a son, a brother, and a friend. I am a Realtor, a partner, and a business owner. I am also a golfer, a lover of the outdoors, a reader, and, most recently, a story teller. Though short, this story details how one powerful idea took root and grew far beyond the small town of Gainesville, Georgia.

Several books have impacted my life, particularly *The Go Giver* by Bob Burg and John David Mann. The *Go Giver* is bylined "A Little Story About a Powerful Business Idea." The book teaches five principles, and having read it through several times, I have tried to live my life by these principles. My business partner, Regina Cochran, and I were given the name of this book by a friend and fellow marketer,

Elizabeth Higgins. We loved its teachings and immediately began implementing them as integral parts of our business practice. Since our initial reading, we have gifted over two hundred copies to our colleagues, friends, and neighbors.

Ideas are very rarely implemented. I am not sure why that is, but it is true. Two years ago I would have laughed at the notion of writing a book to divulge the secrets of my real estate group's business successes, but seven hundred and thirty days later I am about to tell anyone reading this book how implementing a simple idea led to increased visibility, relevance, sales, business success, a scalable business, and a network of influencers.

Today, as I begin to write this book, it is April of 2019. My hope is you will feel these pages have contributed something of value to your personal life, your business life, and even the life of your community. This book is written for anyone who wants to increase their sphere of influence, connections in their community, differentiate themselves among competitors, and make themselves or their business more visible and relevant.

2

CLIMBING THE DOWN ESCALATOR

Climbing anything - a tree, a mountain, or a business - as it falls is not easy to do. We all know how much effort it takes to climb up an escalator that is coming down. You cannot stop or you will lose ground. Not to mention, everyone around you thinks you are crazy. Likewise, going against the flow by trying to build a great business during a terrible economy is just as difficult. External forces pull you groundward, the desire to give up weighs heavy, and there will always be people compelled to drag you down for their own gain. However, climbing alone would make acting against these obstacles near impossible. I am who I am today because of the strength, determination, and faith of my business partner, Regina Cochran. She made a leap of faith by joining me in our climb against the odds. Together, Regina and I also owe much gratitude to our boss and broker, Frank Norton, Jr. Frank blessed our plan and helped our business, the Abernathy Cochran Real Estate Group. We are a residential real estate group located in Gainesville, Hall County, Georgia. Despite beginning our business in the middle of the great recession, we founded our business with a plan: Abernathy Cochran Real Estate Group would be the most positive, most visible, and most relevant group in our market. Visibility and positivity were paramount to us. We wanted to have the positive message about real estate in our community and we wanted everyone to hear and see it. People everywhere were really in the pits during the recession. We have a wonderful community and Regina and I wanted to be a spark and catalyst to improve it and the real estate business within it.

Being positive during The Great Recession was different in and of itself. In the shattered economy, it seemed everyone from journalists to the president had nothing but negativity to offer. If our local newspaper was hard up for stories about some local socialite or another falling from grace, they would reprint grim real estate reports from faraway states like Nevada or California for content.

> *"Susan W---- filed for divorce last week after her husband, Bob W------, was let go from his job at Peach County Bank."*

> *"After their cars were towed away from the city square during business hours last month, Brian and Jane M------- have finally filed for bankruptcy."*

> *"As Employment Opportunities Become More Scarce in Recession, So Does the Middle Class."*

Bad news sold, and it spread like an unavoidable media borne virus. With negativity clouding the market, Regina and I were determined to find the bright spot in every month, quarter, and year because we believed everyone could use a little bit of positivity.

As we began our business together we created a website. From 2009 to 2016, we spent tens of thousands of dollars paying for new designs, search engine optimization, and extra blog sites to build content, keywords, search ranking, and visits. We felt that if we ranked between 1 and 20 for real estate related searches on various search engines, people would find us, see us, and possibly do business with us. Our ultimate goal was this: If anyone in our community was asked to name three real estate agents, we wanted to be included in those three.

This scenario is familiar to any business operating in the Information Age. We wanted our website to be the storefront of our business 24 hours a day, 7 days a week, 365 days a year. It was never closed, but always open and waiting for a potential client to seek real estate expertise.

Amongst other things, our determination to be highly visible was central to the initial success of Abernathy Cochran Group. The positive real estate messages we were generating spread across our community. Our messages were things like this:

- 3.5% more homes sold in Hall County, Georgia, in May of 2010 than in May of 2009.
- Home sales in Hall County, Georgia, during the 3rd quarter of 2010 had an average sales price 8.8% higher than the same time period in 2009.
- The average sales price for a home on Lake Lanier in Hall County has increased each quarter for 7 quarters in a row.

In 2010, our first full year as business partners, Regina and I led our city and county in sales. Much to our surprise, we were humbled to have reached this milestone so quickly after the start of our career together. We have since led our county in Northeast Georgia, one hour north of Atlanta, in real estate sales for each of the last 9 years -- 2010 to present. Despite our success greatly surpassing all expectations, Regina and I were consistently disappointed by our low website traffic

In 2015, after much time and investment, we averaged 568 visits per month online. While many small business owners may insist this is great traffic, Regina and I were fixated on achieving a number much higher than 568. Instead, we strived for 1,000 visits per month on average. It's sound logic: If more people visited us online, more people would want to do business with us, right?

Having a successful business in real estate or any other field requires constant work, generating new ideas, and formulating new strategies. If you are not growing, you are dying. It's as simple as that. According to recent figures from the Georgia Multiple Listing Service, there are 1,860 active real estate agents selling property every year in Hall County, Georgia. Every single one of them wants our business. The Abernathy Cochran Group is their target. They want our listings. They want our buyers. They want our past clients. They have strategies designed to overtake us. They have marketing campaigns designed to shift focus away from the Abernathy Cochran Group and towards their business. A fact in any capitalist economy, our competitors spend thousands of dollars annually to poach our buyers and sellers. If our business is not growing, it is dying.

I absolutely love what I do, but I will say twenty years of providing for a family with an income based in commissioned sales can take its toll. For a career where you can set you own hours, I do not take very much time off. For a loving husband and devoted father, I have been called a workaholic more than I care to admit. This is why I think it so amazing that Abernathy Cochran Group's huge break in expanding our business came because I took a few days off work. While on a five-day spontaneous vacation The Faces of Hall County was born.

3

POUND CAKE

Like many authors before me, I could continue to tell the story of why, how, and what Regina and I did to find financial and personal success with the Abernathy Cochran Group. I could provide all aspects of our actions no matter how insignificant. I could lead directly into the climax of the story and spend the last chapters of this book spinning motivational quotes into a resolution. I could do this, or I could can start with The Faces of Hall County – what actually occurred to transform the business strategy of the Abernathy Cochran Group. So, dessert first. If you ask me—or anyone who knows me for that matter-- there is no better dessert in this world than pound cake. Consider the following list the final product-- a warm, golden brown pound cake—without the hassle of a complicated recipe:

1. Our website traffic jumped 621% in less than 6 months. Our average of 568 visitors per month skyrocketed to 4,096 per month. (The image below shows our website traffic before and after our project began).

(Figure 1. This figure shows a snapshot from Google Analytics showing website visits to the Abernathy Cochran Group website which is where the Faces of Hall County is located. The date range of this snapshot was January 1, 2015, to December 31, 2016. It shows the visit activity on our website before and after we began The Faces of Hall County. The Faces of Hall County began in September of 2015.)

2. The number of real estate sales in our group increased 68% in one year. We closed 91 transaction sides in 2015. In 2016, we closed 153 transaction sides.

3. Our real estate sales volume increased 62% in one year. In 2015, our sales volume was $26,900,000. In 2016, our sales volume was $43,500,000.

4. Within three months of beginning our new project the Greater Hall Chamber of Commerce told us they loved what we are doing and asked if they could link to us on the chamber website. To our knowledge, no other Realtor has ever had a link on our chamber website.

5. Following the implementation of our project in the fall of 2015, people approach me everywhere I go to say they love

what we are doing for our community. People contact us on a weekly basis to commend our work.

6. 2017 and 2018 were the second and third years of our project. In those years, we averaged 5,725 visitors per month on our website. All our visitors were local. Over that two-year period, we had 137,400 visits to our website. We live in a town of 40,000 and a county of 200,000.

7. Our social media pages have thousands of active followers who engage with our posts on a constant basis. Over a one-month period from April to May of 2019, our Facebook posts reached 24,000 people with 14,200 post engagements.

8. Our spheres of influence have grown.

9. Our visibility and influence have risen.

10. In our business, we do numerous things. It is often difficult to pinpoint the exact reason a client chooses to do business with Abernathy Cochran Group. However, we have tracked $175,897 in real estate commissions earned as a direct response (one degree of separation) to our new project.

My partner, Regina Cochran, and I have a combined sixty-three years of experience in the real estate field. In those sixty-three years, we have have tried all manner of avenues to increase our business success. However, nothing has ever garnered more community exposure and financial gain than Faces of Hall County. Over the next several pages, I will share with you the secret to building a successful business no matter your profession. While Abernathy Cochran Group is in the real estate and marketing business, this model can be easily applied to any business where success comes from relationships.

4

BEING GREAT AT WHAT YOU DO

Be great at what you do. It's easier said than done, so I am going to assume that you are already great at what you do. Being a great Realtor, for instance, is the topic of another book. However, when it comes to career fields like real estate, being great at what you do will not necessarily earn you more business. When I do a fantastic job for someone in real estate, my client may be very happy and possibly eternally grateful, but that client may never buy a house again. Odds have it, they will not sell or buy again for 10 years. Maybe I did such a great job that my client tells others about me. While this could be good for some business growth, you should never rely on just this. Some people, no matter how happy you make them, do not have the personality to tell others or sell others about you.

I have been a full time Realtor for twenty-three years. I am very good at what I do, and I absolutely love what I do. If you love what you do, you will never work a day in your life. Unfortunately, being a great Realtor has its drawbacks because everyone thinks they have the skills to become a great Realtor too. I take this as a compliment because my clients not only recognize I am great at my job but that I enjoy it too. I would need more than two hands to count how many of my former clients now have a real estate license. But for every client turned real estate agent, I can also name another client who referred me to a friend and that friend, in turn, closed with me too. A few years go by and one of them is now a Realtor. If you are thinking *He just lost two clients*, you would be right. I did. When a good friend—and my accountant—went through a divorce, he remarried a Realtor. One of my closest business associates and absolute best referral source married the competitor. I am great at what I do, but how can I compete with that? True romance aside, whoever introduced those two took a lot of business from me. And I know who it was. She is now a Realtor, too.

Lastly, in a market saturated by internet agencies and lead capture real estate websites insisting any Realtor can be dubbed the "expert" or "the best agent in town" or the "premium king or queen of real estate," it can be difficult to determine what exactly it means to be great at one's job. Here's the catch: in order to be deemed an "expert," "best agent in town" or "premium king or queen" on these real estate websites, Realtors must pay a monthly fee, a very high monthly fee. To be heralded with the highest accolades these companies offer, a Realtor does not have to have ever lived in the targeted area, to have ever sold anything in the targeted area, or to have any quantifiable expertise in real estate elsewhere. All one has to do is pay money for the endorsement. Because these companies have a prominent online presence, the general public is more apt to trust them and assume they will be put in contact with an expert Realtor despite any evidence of the proper credentials. You may be the very best and want to dismiss paying for the title. When you do dismiss these companies and you see brand new or unsatisfactory agents being promoted, it can be easy to forget this status was bought, not earned. Regina and I found it hard to accept as our market was flooded with internet Realtors. At first, we avoided it all. Then, we joined in by purchasing online recognition for many months. Finally, we decided to try something different. That something different was the Faces of Hall County project.

You cannot rely on just being great alone, and you cannot rely on your current sphere of influence. You must continue making it larger. If your sphere of influence is not growing, it is dying. The most vital part of running a successful local business is current relationships, new relationships, and community engagement.

5

I WAS LATE FOR THE GOLF TRIP

In the summer of 2015, I was invited to attend a golf trip with my best friend, John Canupp, and a couple of acquaintances, Steven Cornett and Robert Cornett. I was not their first choice. I was invited late because their original fourth had to cancel. I said yes to the trip, but as the days quickly approached for me to take time off from work, I did not think I could go. I'll be the first to admit I can be a workaholic. Letting go for a few days in my line of work is not always relaxing. It is hard to let go. In the end, I decided to attend the trip, but because of my nature I joined the trip a day late. A task at work required my direct attention.

Something happened on this trip that started my life and my business on a different path. I was spending time with others and getting to know two new people. I stopped thinking about work and started asking questions about the lives of my two new friends. While beating them all in golf, I was getting to know them. On a course in Saint Simons Island, Georgia, Steven told me about his life as a high school marketing teacher. In his explanation of his high school's work based learning program, he explained several seniors were permitted to leave the school campus on a daily basis in order to gain real world work experience by interning with local businesses. I thought this was interesting.

Then Steven asked me If I could help train a marketing student with my business, and I remember saying, "All I do everyday revolves around marketing. I can certainly teach and train a student in marketing." Two months later, I was contacted by Steven and Gainesville High School's work-based-learning coordinator, Helen Perry. They asked if we would accept Emmeline Jones as a marketing work-based learning intern for the fall semester of 2015. She would be joining us in our offices for three hours per day, five days a week for several months. Emmeline would spend her time working with the Abernathy Cochran Group and in return for her time and efforts we would be grading her work for school credit. What a wonderful opportunity for my group and for the student.

I was then asked if we had a marketing project with which she could assist in one week's time. I had no clue what project we would have ready for Emmeline by her start date, but I said, "Of course. We have a marketing project ready for her to begin, and we can not wait for her to get here next week."

Regina and I began several days of meetings with our social media manager, Ashley Bates. After three days of brainstorming, meetings, computer work, and a stack of heavily marked legal pads we created a marketing project. We decided to promote our community through the many smiling faces of the people who lived or worked in our town. This was and continues to be the message of the project: Our community is much more than the buildings, roads, houses, and shops that dominate our landscape. Our community is defined by its people. We would tell the story of our community through its people one smiling face at a time. We would combine pictures with written questions and answers. People are attracted to positive. People love smiling faces. People are curious about others. Instead of us as Realtors telling everyone why our community is great, we would let the people of our community tell each other and the world why Hall County, Georgia is great.

For our project, we would nominate positive people that lived or worked within our community to be interviewed by us and photographed smiling at the camera. We would ask them fun questions about their lives and loves in our community. We would post the interviews and pictures to a website and share them occasionally to social media pages. All this was done in hopes that our community would read the articles and share them with others. By introducing people to each other or reintroducing them to each other, we would be creating a closer community. In a community like ours, people greet each other with small talk every day, but they hardly know one another. I would bet this is the same everywhere. Every person has a story. We would be the hosts of this unique story. It was our hope in hosting this project on the Abernathy Cochran website that we would have a larger number of local citizens visiting and interacting with one another online. We would call our project and its website *The Faces of Hall County.*

6

CHECKING ALL THE BOXES

As I mentioned earlier, *The Go Giver* has had a large influence on my life and business. Loving a concept, however, does not mean its principles will magically manifest in your life or business. Great ideas die from lack of implementation. Wonderful lessons wither away from lack of application. When creating The Faces of Hall County, we wanted to make certain to check all of the boxes outlined for us in *The Go Giver*:

- Give Value – Give more in value than we take in payment.
- Expand Our Reach – We needed to serve more people and serve them very well.
- Influence – Place the interests of others first throughout this project.
- Be Authentic – We are offering our genuine selves to our community.
- Being Open to Receive –To give effectively, we must remain open to receive.

Establishing Layers of Value

People require four things to survive and thrive in life: shelter, food, water, and attention. In our business and through The Faces of Hall County project, we would commit ourselves to providing two of these four: shelter and attention.

Through The Faces Of Hall County, we choose people (positive people) in our community to meet, interview, and highlight. We created a stage, and we created a spotlight. Whoever we choose is placed on our stage and lit up with our spotlight in front of our community. Through their words and picture of their smiling face we tell part of our community story. When putting them on stage we give them attention. By naming them, one of The Faces of Hall County, we give

FACES OF HALL COUNTY: DR. PEPPER BROWN

March 14, 2016 by Abernathy Carlson Real Estate Group

Dr. Pierpont F. Brown's (Pepper) office is filled with what he calls "relics" (books on surgery) and photos of his family. But some of the prized pieces in his office are the handmade gifts that have been given to him by his children over the years.

Dr. Brown was influenced and inspired by his father, who was the first surgeon in Gainesville, and has a Surgery Pavilion at Northeast Georgia Medical Center named after him.

"I caught the bug at 16 years old when my father used to let me watch surgeries," he said. "He had no idea I would go into medicine, since he passed away while I was still in high school."

Dr. Brown graduated from Gainesville High School, went on to Emory at Oxford, then Emory Medical and did his four year residency at Emory in Augusta before coming home to Gainesville to practice.

We are grateful that Dr. Brown recently took the time to meet with us and answer some questions about his life, interests and love of Hall County.

Question: If you could only eat at one place for an entire week in Hall County, where would it be?

Answer: "Longstreet Café."

Q: How long have you lived in Hall County?

A: "58 years."

Q: If you could travel anywhere in the world right now, where would you go?

A: "Probably England."

Q: What is your favorite social outing in Hall County?

A: "One of my favorites is attending a Gainesville POPS concert."

Q: "What's your favorite book? Or what are you reading now?"

A: "Undaunted Courage (Stephen Ambrose)."

Q: What is your favorite thing about Hall County?

A: "Its home to me."

Q: What is your favorite movie?

A: "Gone With the Wind."

Q: What is your favorite sandwich?

A: "Any that my wife makes."

Q: What former local business makes you the most nostalgic?

A: "The Cake Box."

Q: What advice would you give a crowd of people?

A: "This sounds like a beauty contest question...There's no need to do things you don't want to do. Follow your passion."

Q: When have you felt the most satisfied in your life?

A: "One of the best feelings is giving something and no one knowing you did it, but you and God."

Q: If you could have lunch with anyone in the world, who would you choose?

A: "George Herbert Walker Bush. He would be pretty cool. You've got the politics and he was shot down in WWII. I would love for my father to join us and for us to have our lunch at the Gainesville Botanical Gardens."

The Faces of Hall County is a project to showcase the amazing people that live or work in our community. If you would like to nominate an interesting person to be featured please email pabernathy@gonorton.com

them fame. To some, this is a flash of fame, a quick 15 minutes, but it is so much more than that. This attention lasts for a long time. Every interview we have conducted is on and will permanently stay on The Faces of Hall County website. (Figure 2. This is an example of one of our The Faces of Hall County interviews.) The article posts each have their own url and come up extremely high in search rankings. When searching for the person or their business people are greeted with this wonderful story.

The Faces of Hall County provides a web platform for local citizens to engage with others they know well and those they have yet to meet on the same stage. The audience reads about them and learns about them. The audience may even learn about where they work, or a business they own. The audience interacts online with the Faces of Hall County article. They read it, like it, love it, comment about it, share it with others, and when our "Face" is seen in public, the audience speaks to them, engages with them, and does business with them. Community members provide our Face with attention.

We give value to the people we choose, their families, their businesses and to our community. We take nothing in payment for this. So, for principle one – CHECK.

Expanding Reach

The Faces of Hall County is a fantastic way to meet anyone we want to in our community. Real estate coaches, trainers, teachers, speakers, and brokers will tell you to go out in public and hand someone your business card. They will tell you to ask them, "Do you know someone who would like to buy or sell a house?" Ask them, "Will you keep my card and call me when you are ready to buy or sell?" Ask them, "Will you please pass along my card to someone you know who needs a Realtor?" They will tell you to knock on doors and introduce yourself. They will tell you to hand out a giveaway like a calendar or recipe or flower seed packet or newsletter. While a potential client with a peanut allergy might not need a recipe for peanut butter cookies, at least an effort was made to meet a possible seller in the community. All of these strategies are in an effort to meet new people and try to sell to them.

Stop doing this.

Larry Kendall's book *Ninja Selling* is also a favorite book of mine. I highly recommend it as the best philosophy on selling I have ever studied. Giving value to and being connected to others is at the core of Ninja Selling and similarly the Faces of Hall County. I have not yet had the pleasure of meeting Larry Kendall, but I have been to trainings with one of his certified program coaches. Her name is Clara Capano. Clara is the best instructor I have had in my twenty-three year career. In addition to being an instructor for Ninja Selling, Clara is an author, a master coach, and is a part of the Forbes Coaches Council. She is an inspiration and part of the reason I decided to write this book. Soft selling is one of the concepts Larry and Clara teach.

This is how The Faces of Hall County allows us to meet new people:

In my town I can walk up to anyone and say, "Hello. My name is Brad Abernathy. What is your name?"

"Hello, Brad. My name is Joe."

"Hey, Joe. I am a local Realtor, and I am the creator and host of The Faces of Hall County. We promote our community through the people of our community one face at a time. If you are willing, I would love to promote you as one of The Faces of Hall County by asking you a few questions about your life here and what you love about our town. I will include your picture and even some information about your business here. Would that be ok with you?"

Remember: Almost everyone loves and craves attention. My conversation with Joe is all about Joe. The questions I ask Joe are about Joe, his family and friends, his occupation, things he loves to do and dreams of doing, things he likes about our community, and places he loves in our community. Lastly, I ask Joe to nominate someone positive who would make a great Face of Hall County, and I also ask him what three words or phrases come to mind when he hears the word "home". Joe leaves me with his name, number, home address, email address and signature on a release allowing me to use his information in our project. I tell Joe to visit our website to see other Faces of Hall County, ask him to follow us on social media so he is able to view his interview once it is posted, and ask him to share the post featuring his interview across his preferred social media platforms.

Which is a better way of adding someone to your sphere of influence? Selling and soliciting someone with your card and asking for their business, or providing that person with recognition, attention, and local fame? It is completely obvious which way is better for Joe. How about which way is better for you?

I have just made Joe's day, week, and month. Joe will love the recognition and attention The Faces of Hall County gives him. If Joe has a business, Joe's business receives more exposure in the community, too. Regina and I at Abernathy Cochran Group stay in touch with Joe from this point forward. He has been added to our sphere of influence. By giving value to Joe, we have expanded our reach by several, because Joe likely has family, friends, and employees or coworkers who have now heard of Abernathy Cochran Group.

According to Larry Kendall, author of *Ninja Selling*, "If some-one feels they are being sold, they will want to get away. If you listen carefully to them, you will be successful. Get engaged with people. Learn about them. Be a servant to them. Offer them value."

Our reach expands with each interview. So, for principle two – CHECK.

Influence

For a community project to truly work, we had to care more about the people of our project than anything else. And we do. We spend time with the people we interview for The Faces of Hall County, and the attention we give to them is genuine. Every single time we promote a new Face of Hall County, we are wishing for the best for that person. If that person owns a business, we want our community to support and engage with that business. If that person works with a charity, we hope more community members will get involved just from being introduced. As always, our goal is to promote the person. Because of our work with The Faces of Hall County, we have featured restaurant owners whose establishments have subsequently run out of food because of the publicity boost. We have featured community members who earned more jobs and clients because of the added exposure. Results like these make this project important. We frequently hear news of results like these, and this is what makes our project so special.

Even though we have only been conducting this project for less than four years, people have been motivated to achieve their goals and dreams because of its influence. One interviewee said, "I could not give up on my goals because so many people read the article and held me accountable."

The interests of others are central to The Faces of Hall County. So, for principle three – CHECK.

Authenticity

As we have continued to expand The Faces of Hall County project over the past three and a half years, many have asked us, "What will you do once you have interviewed every citizen in your small community?" Others ask it a different way when they say, "Aren't there only so many people you can include?" Still others will ask us why we are wasting our time interviewing a subject for The Faces of Hall County who will probably never need a Realtor to help them buy or sell property.

These questions could be used as a simple litmus test for a truly authentic community project. We wanted something real and not something similar to a "who's who" list of our community. Our project set out to tell the story of our community, told through our people, one face at a time. We are not a "who's who" or a "forty under forty" list. We do not just include very active real estate buyers and sellers. We look for positive members of our community, and that is it.

We know we will never receive real estate business from most of the people included in The Faces of Hall County. We will however, and have, received increased real estate business from people who read, love, and follow this truly authentic community project. Each member of The Faces of Hall County contributes to our woven community story, and we would have it no other way.

This project is authentic in every way. For principle four – CHECK.

Open to Receive

The Go-Giver asserts to effectively give, you must be open to receive. We are open to receive. We do not give with the need or desire to receive in our minds. We are open when it comes. This project was never about the financial numbers. It was never our intention to begin The Faces of Hall County and stop it after a month or two if we didn't see any added financial gains. Abernathy Cochran Group conducts this project because it gives value to the people in our community. It makes people happy. It impacts their lives and businesses. The feeling we get for creating this happiness and energy is amazing. Any added perks in our personal or business lives stemming from this project are bonuses.

Whether it be influence, an award nomination, increased business, or unforeseeable opportunities, we are open to receive whatever this project brings. For principle five, being open to receive – CHECK.

7

PROJECTIONS AND REALITY

For six years before The Faces Of Hall County, Regina and I worked very hard to increase our online website visits. We knew each visit to our website was a chance to make a great impression on the visitor. If the project site were branded correctly, if there was a captivating web presence, if the site engaged the visitor, maybe this visitor would choose to do real estate business with Abernathy Cochran Group.

In the first quarter of 2015, the highest volume of web traffic we averaged was 568 per month. Our projections for what The Faces of Hall County would produce were very hopeful. We thought if we could be disciplined enough to meet and interview at least two community members per week and to post those interviews online shortly after, we could reasonably attract 100 new web visitors a week. The breakdown of 50 online visits per Faces interview post seemed reasonable. If this could be achieved we would finally meet my goal of 1,000 visits per month to our company website, an increase of 75%.

We believed our projections were right, what we were doing for others was right, what we were doing for our community was right, but a 75% increase was a lofty goal.

We started The Faces of Hall County in the fall of 2015. We were disciplined in both interviewing two community members per week and posting two interviews online per week. All of the feedback we encountered as we began this project was unbelievably positive. People contacted us to nominate community members, people stopped us out in public to say how much they loved reading the articles, and people were sharing these articles on social media every day. But, could we increase our traffic as we hoped?

The answer is YES. And the results far exceeded any number we ever contemplated. The amount of visits to our website in the first quarter of 2016 were 621% higher than the first quarter of 2015. We moved our average visits per month from 568 to 4,096 in less than six months. The 4,096 website visits included 5,856 page views per month. This means that while we were able to get over 4,000 visits per month to the website, they looked at over 5,800 pages on our website per month. Every new visitor drawn to our company by The Faces of Hall County was also viewing our company's branded website, our names in association with the company, information about our real estate business, and homes we had for sale.

Our Business Principles

Early in this book, I talked about how The Faces of Hall County would have the five major principles of *The Go-Giver* integrated into its basic framework. While the project clearly meets the standards outlined in *The Go-Giver*, how does it match with the business goals for Abernathy Cochran Real Estate Group?

To Be More Visible:

1. The Faces of Hall County brought thousands more people to our website. To approximate, over 225,000 visitors were attracted to our website in a little less than four years because of this project.

2. On a monthly basis, several people contact us with nominations for community members they would like to see featured on our website.

3. Our Facebook followers jumped from a couple hundred to over 2,700.

4. Our Instagram followers skyrocketed from dozens to over 1,300.

5. People talked about this project everywhere Regina and I went.

6. The Greater Hall County Chamber of Commerce loved The Faces of Hall County so much they asked for our permission to feature on the chamber website.

To Be More Relevant:

1. Within a few short weeks, Abernathy Cochran Group was a frequent topic of conversation across our community.

2. Gainesville High School provided the first student internship for this project. Now other high schools wanted to send us interns to assist with the project.

3. We had community members' photos, names, and interviews on our website. We also had several local businesses mentioned on our website.

4. As the new sales leaders in our market as well as the unofficial ambassadors and promoters of our community, Abernathy Cochran became incredibly relevant. Since The Faces of Hall County began, members of Abernathy Cochran Group have been asked to join several community groups, boards or directors, community advisory committees, and civic, school, and church leadership groups.

8

WHAT DO THE PEOPLE OF HALL COUNTY, GEORGIA SAY?

"I am Pepper Brown, and I am a general surgeon here in Gainesville, Georgia. The Faces of Hall County really does promote the community. I have seen a lot of people on this particular program who I knew of or did not personally know well. I was able to see a different side of them, and I was also able to put a face with a name. It makes it more like a hometown rather than a bunch of individuals in a city."

Dr. Pepper Brown

General Surgeon

Northeast Georgia Physicians Group

* * *

"What a way to step outside of what you normally do and what your business is about. You are not just selling homes, you are saying, "Okay, yes, we have this to offer, but our community has something to offer, and we need to bring that to light." Gainesville is a community with so much history. And it has so many people who are diamonds in the rough, and you are bringing these people to light. I do follow The Faces of Hall County because I want to see who you think are the pillars of Hall County, and I want to see what they are bringing to this community."

Zandrea Stephens

Division Manager, Frances Meadows Aquatic Center

City of Gainesville Parks and Recreation Department

* * *

"Love what you all do. You see I copy a lot and share through The Greater Hall Chamber of Commerce Vision 2030 Project to show others the amazing people in our community.

Elizabeth Higgins

Vision 2030, Executive Director

Greater Hall County Chamber of Commerce

* * *

"What a great honor for me to be asked to be a small part of this beautiful project. At the beginning, I was not fully aware of its overall intention, but I feel a special connection with the individuals whose lives have been highlighted. I am humbled that I was included among those who show that the diversity of our community is our strength. We're more of a GREAT bunch because of strong ones like you who emphasize the positive threads that make all of us COMMUNITY. Merci beaucoup for asking me to contribute."

Myrtle Figueras

Former Mayor and Councilwoman

City of Gainesville, Georgia

* * *

"I loved being part of The Faces of Hall County. I received wonderful responses and, because I know of it, I am able to look and read about other people who are in the project. I truly believe it makes a large community feel smaller with a more hometown feel. Thank you so much for letting me be a part of something so cool."

Amanda Browning

Owner Amanda's Farm to Fork

Lula, Georgia

* * *

"I feel this project, The Faces of Hall County, is an amazing experience for our students, school, and the Work Based Learning Program of Flowery Branch High School. I hope it continues, and we are able to place a student for the 2nd semester of the 2018-2019 school year to help you conduct interviews and write posts for the south end of the county. We have some really great people in our community, and this project showcases that. Kudos to you for providing a "small town" feeling via a professional platform for our community leaders and representatives to be recognized. Please let me know if you have any other opportunities for our school or our students to be involved in. I am grateful for your partnership."

Christy Carter

Work Based Learning Coordinator

Flowery Branch High School

Flowery Branch, Georgia

* * *

"I was very happy to have been asked to be a Face of Hall County. My business was very new, and the exposure I received was amazing. I have also loved following this project on Instagram to learn about and meet new people who I might not have normally met. God has moved in big ways for me since starting this business, and your project was part of that. Thank you for spreading the word about me and my business."

Landon Brockmeyer

The Hot Dog Ninja

Gainesville, Georgia

* * *

"I was honored to be asked to be a part of this wonderful community 'get to know your neighbors' type of literature – online. I love reading the interviews and hearing the different opinions of everyone. I've learned about businesses that I'd never been to before. I also love getting to know the PEOPLE of our great community. I love how EASY it is to read online. I love the VARIETY of leaders, business owners, and others who make up the project."

Heidi Ferguson

Homemaker

Gainesville, Georgia

9

VALUE TO STUDENTS

At the beginning of this story, I told you The Faces of Hall County was created as a marketing project in anticipation of the high school senior, Emmeline Jones, who was beginning an internship with us. We would be doing this project with or without outside help, but the project started because of an internship, and we have worked with high school interns every semester since the project's inception.

As you may have guessed, a high school student might not be well skilled in face-to-face communication with adults. However, Emmeline was eager to learn. At the start of her internship, Emmeline observed Regina and I as we interviewed community members for The Faces of Hall County. She listened, asked some follow-up questions, took notes, and wrote several of our interviews. As she grew more confident, we allowed her to set up, conduct, and write her own interviews. She loved it!

With Emmeline's assistance and dedication to the project, The Faces of Hall County was an enormous success. Emmeline asked her high school work based learning counselor if she could join us again for her last semester of high school, and everyone at our company unanimously agreed. Two other high schools in our community were interested in what we were doing and offered student interns for work with The Faces of Hall County. Since we began The Faces of Hall County in the fall of 2015, fourteen marketing, journalism, and business student interns have worked with us from three different high schools.

The list of skills interning seniors have gained from working with Abernathy Cochran Group is lengthy, and we are proud to have supported student growth in the following areas:

- Interpersonal communication
- Understanding expectations for professional attire
- Proper business etiquette
- Conducting thorough interviews
- Listening and note taking
- Advertising and marketing
- Creative writing
- Grasping the importance of marketing, web marketing, and social media marketing
- Promoting the importance of audience engagement as it relates to marketing
- Preparing for the challenges of communication, marketing, and competition in the real world of business

As we continue to grow in Northeast Georgia, we have decided to create The Faces of Jackson County. Jackson County is a neighboring county to Hall, and Abernathy Cochran Group does significant business in this community, too. When approaching the Jackson County community, my first stop was Jefferson High School. I hoped we would be able to share how we were working with students in

Hall County in order to secure possible interns who would be willing to assist with The Faces of Jackson County.

The teachers and administrators loved my presentation more than I expected. They asked if I would allow an entire marketing and entrepreneurship class to work on The Faces of Jackson County project for class credit. Wow! Everything we do with this project exceeds our expectations.

In preparation for the Faces of Jackson County, I was asked to teach the basic concepts of real estate and the importance of marketing relationships, word-of-mouth advertising… to the class of seniors who would be assisting me with the project. I also taught them the difference in salaried professions and commission based professions. The students were engaged and eager to make this brand new community project a success. In the first month after we launched, over 2,000 people visited *The Faces of Jackson County* website. Though geared towards the Jackson County community, Abernathy Cochran Real Estate remained the creator and host of the project.

Three of the Jefferson High School students were members of Future Business Leaders of America (FBLA). They asked my permission to enter this student/business cooperation project in an FBLA marketing competition. Of course I agreed and I coached them through their project by giving charts and website analytics data along with more information. Their project progressed to the state of Georgia finals and won third place. As one of the top three finishers in the state, they were invited to compete in the national finals in San Antonio, Texas in July of 2019.

Several school systems around the state of Georgia have now heard about The Faces of and are communicating with our office now to see how they can get involved. I cannot wait to see what unfolds with student involvement. Stay tuned.

I recently asked Emmeline Jones to send me a note about her time with Abernathy Cochran Group. This is what she said:

"During senior year of high school, I had the opportunity to work with Brad Abernathy on the Faces of Hall County project. I interviewed citizens of the Hall County community about their personal lives, passions, and professions. The interviewees ranged from business men to local artists. In order to formulate the perfect interview topics, each question underwent several developmental stages. We wanted to profile people's business endeavors and their contributions to the community but also give them a chance to show their personalities. I have always found people very interesting, so this project was perfect for me. Having grown up in Gainesville, Georgia, this opportunity granted me a new appreciation for my hometown because I was able to see the members of my community in a new light. Gainesville, Georgia may be a small town, but it does not have a shortage of outstanding citizens.

Working on this project helped me decide I wanted to major in Communications at The College of Charleston in Charleston, South Carolina. I am beginning my senior year at The College this fall, and my studies have taught me much about the art of communicating. However, in all my academic career, the Faces of Hall County project gave me the most hands on experience. I have a new understanding of the project because I am now able to retrospectively recognize and apply communications theories to the Faces of Hall County. I am grateful for the chance to work with Brad, Regina, and other members of their group, Rosemary Hancock and Ashley Bates, and to develop instrumental skills in communications before college. I love learning about people and exploring ways to help us better explain one another. The Faces of Hall County project has surpassed my wildest expectations, and I'm very happy I was able to help start it and watch it grow."

Emmeline Jones

Former The Faces of Hall County Intern

Charleston, South Carolina

10

ARE DEEP COMMUNITY ROOTS NECESSARY?

Could The Faces of Hall County have been just as successful for someone without deep community roots? Are long-time community roots needed to be an effective host for The Faces Of? Deep roots or no roots, it does not matter. This project will allow your business to outperform all competitors in your area regardless. Why? People love attention.

A study was done a few years ago in California by the Hobbs & Herder Marketing Firm. I first read about this study in Larry Kendall's book *Ninja Selling*. Hobbs & Herder surveyed homeowners in a neighborhood and asked one question: "If you were to sell your home, which Realtor would you call?" They recorded the results and ranked the Realtors mentioned based on this top-of-mind awareness. Then the researchers created a fictional Realtor and sent members of this neighborhood mailers from him each week for eight weeks. After the eight week mailing campaign was completed, Hobbs & Herder returned to survey the neighborhood with the same question. Upon asking, the new results showed the most named Realtor was the fictional Realtor—a Realtor who did not even exist. You do not need deep roots to make an impact on people and succeed – just exposure.

Imagine if I was a stranger in a new town. For argument's sake, let us move my family from Gainesville, Georgia to Lafayette, Louisiana. I know no one in my new town. We will pretend my real estate license is valid in the state of Louisiana as well. I could start paying a real estate lead capture site to be a favorite agent in Lafayette. I could even be dubbed "the star agent" or something similar to it if I paid enough. (Never you mind I would need a GPS to drive from one listing to the next, and I have never sold a house in Lafayette.) These websites cost thousands of dollars per year to join and do not really tell the truth about who the market experts really are. Don't do it.

Instead, what if I had started The Faces of Lafayette? I would start looking for happy local citizens and business owners to speak to and interview in Lafayette instead of Hall County. I could tell the citizens of Lafayette I am a local Realtor and creator of a wonderful community project I want them to be a part of. I could even be 100% honest and tell them I am brand new to town and am doing this project to gain a better understanding of the Lafayette community. I could tell them I decided to create and host The Faces of Lafayette as a way for my family to get to know this community one face at a time, and others in this community would be introduced or reintroduced to the great people of this town as they follow its progression. I want to learn the positive story of this community one interview at a time, and I will be allowing others to experience Lafayette through the lens of an excited newcomer.

Being new to town, I would set a goal for myself to meet two people per day. And remember, I would be meeting them but also giving them value and making them feel noticed. Two people per day, five days per week, equals ten people per week and five hundred twenty people per year. In just a few months, I would have given value to hundreds of citizens, met hundreds of people, compiled an amazing list of names, home and email addresses, cell phone numbers, and promoted hundreds of people and dozens of businesses. There is no end to The Faces of Lafayette. Before long, I am in constant flow with more people in Lafayette than any other Realtor in town. The personal relationships I am building with the people of Lafayette are worth so much more for long term business and personal success than buying leads online.

Within a few months, I have built incredible visibility. I have thousands of visitors to my brand new website. I have hundreds of people in my new sphere of influence. I have instant credibility. I have the ability to make connections in a new town. I can certainly assure any of you reading this that other Realtors in Lafayette will soon be saying something very similar to: "Who is this new guy? Where did he come from?"

11

4,500 MILES, TWO $5,000 CHECKS, AND A LEGAL PAD

Extraordinary is the first word of this book. I will now tell you about an extraordinary series of events, a few conversations, and a leap of faith that changed many lives, including my own. I now know exactly how to give value through The Faces of Hall County. Could I give value to others outside of my county?

In 2017, The Faces of Hall County was eighteen-months-old and growing. It was viral on social media in a hyper local way. Many were taking notice—including my competitors. The Faces of Hall County was being shared on other websites and our own chamber of commerce featured it on their media outlets. While at a student awards ceremony someone introduced a keynote speaker by quoting something the speaker had said in her Faces of Hall county interview from the year previous. We were sometimes beating our own local newspaper to the scoop with some interviews. We joke about it around our offices: The absolute best way to be interviewed by our local newspaper is to be featured as one of The Faces of Hall County first.

Conversation #1:

A friend of mine, Corey, whom I have known since the mid-1980s was a Realtor in another town about an hour from mine. He watched what we were doing from a far and loved it. He wanted to know everything about it: the secrets, the numbers behind the scenes, the business relationships we were generating from it—everything. He wanted me to teach him how to start a similar project in his own community. He knew that I had, most likely, encountered yet maneuvered around road blocks along the way, and he was hoping I would teach him.

Real estate can be a very lonely business. Before Regina and I created the Abernathy Cochran Group, I was on my own. I lived the life of the lone Realtor from 1996 to 2009. Anyone working in this industry knows you cannot trust many people in our business. You cannot tell them your business secrets. You cannot tell anyone what you are planning to do. You cannot tell others what property you might list for sale. Real estate is a cutthroat business.

This may sound crazy to some of you, but any seasoned Realtor working in a relatively small town will understand my next statement: There have been numerous times through the years I would park my vehicle deep in a driveway when I visited a new potential listing. When the vehicle of a visible small-town Realtor is parked in front of your house, people talk. I can hear it now. *Brad's Tahoe was parked at Sarah's T---'s house this afternoon. Do you think they are about to sell? Why would they be leaving the neighborhood? Do you think her mom is sick again, and they are moving to Florida to help? Did her husband lose his job?*

Though my efforts to seem covert may sound insane to some, I only say these things to demonstrate just how foreign sharing my business secrets with anyone has become. My old friend wanted to know what I was doing with The Faces of Hall County and how he could do it as well. Well, I would never tell.

Conversation #2:

While walking the sidewalks and browsing through the shops of downtown Paia (population 2,668) on the island of Maui in Hawaii, I turned into the local Coldwell Banker Real Estate office. I began a conversation with a local Realtor named Rhonda Smith-Sanchez. We shared thoughts about her market in Hawaii and mine in Georgia. Suffices it to say, Maui and Gainesville are not the same real estate markets. We may have waterfront homes on Lake Lanier, but a property with an ocean view in Hawaii is certainly another story. However, despite our market differences, it turned out our experience and successes in business were similar. We did not compete in the same market and would probably never see each other again. (As of the writing of this book, Rhonda and I have never spoken again. She will, however, get a copy of this soon and I can only hope it finds her very well!) Because our offices were 4,500 miles apart, I felt comfortable divulging the details of The Faces of Hall County with Rhonda. She told me about some things she does to market herself in real estate, and I told her about the success of The

Faces of Hall County. She said she thought it was a wonderful idea. It could be done there, too.

On the flight home from Maui, I could not stop thinking about Corey and Rhonda. If I helped Corey start The Faces of his community and he did what I taught him to do, he would be successful. He would rise in visibility and influence. If I helped Rhonda do the same thing for The Faces of Paia and she did what I taught her, she would continue to be highly successful, and her business would grow. I would have a partner in Corey's town and in Rhonda's town. I would be connected to influencers in two other communities, and they would be connected to each other through me. Corey, Rhonda, and I could share ideas, lessons, experiences, and successes. We might even have business referrals we could share with one another.

For those who know me, there is usually a pen behind my ear and a yellow legal pad in my computer bag. (I go through several legal pads every month). Of course, I had one with me on a vacation to Hawaii. I was writing notes, thoughts, and ideas furiously for the duration of that flight home.

I called Corey soon thereafter. I told him several things he wanted to know. I told him that I would be willing to tell him everything so he could recreate The Faces of Hall County in his market for $5,000.

I knew The Faces of Hall County model was well worth the money. We have several sales per year directly from this project. In the first year alone after we started our project our sales increased by sixteen million dollars. I was asking him for less than he would make on one sale. I waited to see what he would say, and when he answered, he did not hesitate. He sent me a check for $5,000 right away, and I gave up the secrets to the best business idea I have ever had or seen in practice in my industry anywhere.

The anticipation of The Faces Of Corey's community drove me crazy. I was hoping it would start right away so I could watch his success. However, that did not happen. Our first launch never got off the ground before it imploded. The daily grind of life, poor communication with an outsourced web developer, among other things caused implementation to stall. Nothing happened. My old friend was frustrated, and it was all in his hands. I could not in good conscience keep his money, so I refunded him a $5,000 check. I thanked him very much for the thought, for his trust, and for his initiative. I would figure out a different marketing strategy and get back to him one day.

I returned to the legal pad.

When my friend was in charge of his own The Faces of project, I had no control and no great way to help. Instead of giving everything to someone and trusting that they implement it the right way, I could do it for them. I could give someone a project site branded toward their business and their community, and I could make it look great. If I managed The Faces Of Community sites from a 30,000 foot level, I could update them whenever needed, add new technology when needed, help secure them for privacy, keep them looking and functioning the same way for the growing brand, and possibly tie them together in an extended network some day. Costs for partners would drop because I would change the business model from a large investment up front to a small up front charge and a recurring monthly fee for the partner's use of the site. I would stay connected to each partner to coach them along the way, offer insights and assistance when needed, and share ideas and strategies currently working for us and others. One day we would have several partners with futures much brighter than our own, and they would be able to offer us ideas of significant value in order to improve our collective business.

The Faces of Company was born from the lessons we learned from our first attempt to spread this business. There is no success without failure. When we originally began the project, it was never our intent to share the idea. However, other businessmen and women in the community were frequently curious about it. It was on my flight home from Maui when I decided this business idea was one I could no longer keep to myself. If we are giving incredible value to the people of our community, we could give value to people in other communities as well. We could share this with a partner in every town in my state, in this country, and beyond. We would give each of our partners the tools to conduct their own The Faces Of project on a silver platter. We would help our partners succeed by giving their businesses added value, and they would, in turn, give value to the people of their communities.

This is how the journey to this book began.

12

THE FACES OF COMPANY

After the eye opening realization we could create exponential value for other businesses through franchise partnerships, Regina and I began the search for a strategic partner. After a lengthy search process, we chose Angie Veugeler of Veugeler Design Group in Buford, Georgia for all our web designing needs. She and her staff are highly creative, have fantastic experience in web development, and were positive they could help The Faces Of grow on a larger scale. More importantly, they believed in what we were offering others.

During our fifth meeting at Veugeler, a new face joined the conference table. His name was Brian Weiss, Vice President of Sales and Head of Business Development for Veugeler. During that first meeting, Brian's enthusiasm towards the project was both promising and distracting. It was almost as if a Mexican jumping bean was seated across from me at the table. I could see his energy level was high. He could not sit still! Of course, I could tell he wanted to discuss The Faces of project, but he tried his best to listen before launching into the talk. Finally, when he could not keep quiet any longer, Brian had to share his excitement for our business with the rest of the conference table. His energy and commitment that day and since have been very valuable to me.

Here are Brian's thoughts from that first project meeting at Veugeler Design Group:

"A requirement in business is growth. Additional resources created from growth are used to make improvements in the business, add additional team members, learn new skills, innovate an offering or process, etc. Growth is critical. With that, velocity in growth is aided by specialization. When it's crystal clear who your customer is and why you serve them better than anybody else, growth can happen in a consistent, predictable, and sustainable way. I have been in sales for more than fifteen years. The very first time I heard Brad Abernathy explain what he was doing with The Faces of Hall County, I was immediately very excited. How does a Realtor create specialization and differentiate themselves in their market? Real Estate is a highly competitive business and the home buyer/seller doesn't generally buy or sell that frequently. How can a Realtor establish a brand as a true community leader and create genuine influence as a specialist?"

"That's what struck me about The Faces of Hall County. Through this project, Brad was providing himself permission to connect with virtually any community member he wishes because of his desire to promote them as an important member of their great community. This is a very important first chance to make an impression, and it's memorable for the person he meets. One interview at a time, Brad is growing his sphere of influence and local reputation as "the guy" in the community. The almost 8,000 monthly visits to their websites and 2,700+ followers on social media see Brad connecting and telling the story of people all over the community. In time, they come to realize, who knows Gainesville and Hall County better than Brad Abernathy? That is a critical element to the success of this project. Brad has achieved specialization as the market leader, and he did it without focusing on Real Estate but focusing on the people and giving value first. I loved everything about The Face Of from the moment I heard the story."

When asked why he thought The Faces Of would be valuable to others, Brian said this:

"This project was inspired by the book *The Go-Giver*. Brad is a testament to the benefit of giving to others, and he does so without keeping score. The law of reciprocity suggests you will gain so much more in return. With The Faces Of, we are creating a community of professionals who see the benefit of this idea. We're partnering with people in markets all over the country who are creating closer communities where they live and recognizing significant gains both in community influence and business growth. These partners are now part of the greater The Faces Of network where we're fostering idea sharing and support in our pursuit to be the best version of ourselves. This project works and our partners are witnessing the gravity of it in their markets. It provides so many opportunities to engage with the community in different ways and to help lift others up. The great thing is, with so many partners leveraging the same project in their market, it will only add value to our partners. We're all encountering different ways to leverage this platform for good and by having a peer group to share it with, everybody is better off. We're setting out to create a celebration of community from coast to coast and, in doing so, are contributing to the growth of top producing partners along the way."

Brian Weiss

Vice President of Sales

Veugeler Design Group

Buford, Georgia

Today, our company is growing. To thank for that, we have a great idea, a great business team, and a core purpose to spread value through collaboration. We offer franchise partnerships to one person, company, or business group per community. We provide the website and the necessary tools to assure anyone can begin The Faces Of project in their community. Our franchise partners pay a modest up front charge for initial setup and then a recurring monthly partnership fee for as long as they remain in business with The Faces Of. We are now a network of influencers. Each of us is connected to very visible and relevant network of influencers in sixty one communities in fifteen states across the country – as of this writing. We share business referrals and ideas with one another across state lines. So far, our mix of partners includes Realtors, insurance agents, medical consultants, marketers, website design companies, and real estate brokerages.

The Faces Of is a vehicle to deliver value. Our plan is guaranteed to make any given business highly visible and relevant in any given community. Our team at The Faces Of will help them on exactly how to do that.

13

WHAT DO OUR PARTNERS SAY?

"In the two short weeks since I launched this project, I am being sought out to write stories about people I have not met yet. They are my new friends. As I am in the business of making friends, The Faces of Houston County has helped me foster friendships with people who may have otherwise remained strangers. I have a new listing appointment and a new buyer directly from this project. People are scrambling to get their interviews completed so they can be the next one promoted."

Sylvia Moore Myers

Realtor, NextHome Realty

Faces of Houston County, Georgia

* * *

"I am having a lot of fun conducting the Faces Of interviews for my project in Florida. I'm hooked. It's a really cool idea and experience. I find the face time you get with those you interview is invaluable. The questions we ask are lighthearted enough to not intimidate, but they make the subject stop and think. Sitting there recording everything, you can just watch their reactions and expressions, truly listening to them and making them feel heard. I'm addicted. I met the mayor tonight and lined up an interview with him on Friday of this week."

Alex Bittner

Realtor, Adams Cameron Real Estate

The Faces of East Volusia, Florida

* * *

"The process of interviewing individuals has been so much more rewarding than I ever expected. I have thoroughly enjoyed conducting these interviews as they have led to some of the best conversations I've had. I almost forget what it is that I am there to accomplish. People have been very receptive to the idea. It's like their fifteen minutes of fame. The networking opportunities are endless. I can't wait to see what unfolds. Once I went live with the project, the feedback and interaction were instantaneous. I had emails and phone calls within minutes of my first live posting."

Rachel Marascalco

Realtor

The Faces of St. Simons, Georgia

* * *

"I have been a Realtor for twenty years and a franchise partner with The Faces Of for a few months. The Faces Of is now our primary marketing platform. We have reduced our other forms of marketing materials. The one-on-one contact from this platform is one hundred times more powerful than a postcard. We are in the relationship business first and just happen to sell real estate. Hands down, this is the most brilliant idea we have come across. As we build the website, we are noticing more and more of the general public nominating people for us to interview. It is taking on a life of its own. We are meeting some great folks in our community who we never knew before the start of this project. Our business is heavily based upon referrals, and this will become a gold mine for us. We have a segment of our database now labeled 'The Faces of Henry'. Our goal is to get in touch with these folks once a month. We have made these people feel good by sharing their story via social media. Because they feel good, they have a sense of giving back to us (a.k.a. referrals). If you want to grow your database with A+ people, then this is the absolute best and fastest way to build a critical mass of high quality people. These are people who will want to refer to you and, at the same time, build your brand on social media by making you more recognizable, not just as a realtor, but as an ambassador of the community."

Scott Patrick

Realtor, Keller Williams

The Faces of Henry County, Georgia

* * *

I sincerely hope our partners have found value and visibility with The Faces Of project because we are honored to support them as their businesses continue to grow and flourish.

14

GUIDANCE FROM ME

If you have ever played on a sports team in your life, Little League included, you know there are very few coaches who have put their warmup drills, detailed plays, and motivational speeches into action off the field. While I am no coach myself, I will tell you right now I do not have all of the answers, but I can advise and point you in the right direction. Why? Because I do real estate and marketing every single day. Whether you are a Realtor, a restaurant owner, or an aspiring politician, the principles in this book, if applied to your business, will make you successful.

Stop right here. Let's back up. Am I telling a restaurant owner using the principles of this book will make him or her more successful? Yes. Could an owner of a diner in Wichita, Kansas be the host of The Faces of Wichita and actually succeed from it? Absolutely. What do a restaurant owner and a Realtor have in common? Everything. They both serve people.

Let me explain. For argument's sake, I will assume, again, the restaurant owner is already great at what he does. Imagine if every day of the week Jason, the owner of Wichita Diner and the host of The Faces of Wichita, invited someone positive from his community to join him for a free lunch and a quick interview. Jason would join the interviewee for lunch, ask her a few questions for The Faces Of project, and take her picture with the restaurant as a backdrop. The interviewee leaves happy and honored. She is honored with the local fame, and Jason has a new client. He has great new content for his community story. He has thousands of followers every month on his website. His sphere of influence is now remarkable. He might even display all of these pictures on his walls. Because The Faces of Wichita is housed in Jason's restaurant, his business is certain to attract more customers.

One of the wonderful things about being a part of The Faces Of is meeting influencers. I have travelled the same routes and paths daily for most of my life, and in doing so, I have failed to notice all of the influencers along the way. An influencer is defined as a person who can influence another. I also like to define these people as connectors. They do not necessarily stand out from those around them, and they don't wear name badges to announce their presence among us. As the host of our local The Faces of Hall County, my influence within the community began to rise. As my influence rose, I began to notice others around me who were connectors, and they noticed me.

Now that I am an open book, I would like to review the secrets to my success. First, read *The Go-Giver* by Bob Burg and John David Mann and *Ninja-Selling* by Larry Kendall. Second, join us as a partner for The Faces Of. *The Go-Giver* will put you in the correct frame of mind for personal and business growth and success. The Faces Of will give you visibility, relevance, and a vast sphere of influence.

Ninja Selling will then instruct you how to always remain relevant within your sphere of influence.

Being a franchise partner with The Faces Of gives you (1) velocity and (2) confidence. (3) Our partners will not only immediately benefit from our resources, but the learning curves for a new user will also be minimal.

Micki in Augusta started interviewing the day after she became a partner. She didn't need to hire a web developer or generate her own site map and budget. She did not have to think through the logistics of reaching out, setting up an interview, formatting the questions for an interview, posting an interview online in a timely manner, or promoting an interview via social media. She was able to get started on The Faces of Augusta with no hassle. Micki was also confident The Faces of Augusta would be successful because I and all of our other partners are testimonies to the strengths of this marketing strategy. That confidence is important in helping partners see this project through. A partnership with The Faces Of guarantees any business owner will significantly increase their community presence and sphere of influence while undoubtedly growing their business.

Partners also receive the benefit of joining a (4) peer group of like-minded professionals who aspire to be successful regardless of their field. It's our own private mastermind group. Micki, for example, immediately became The Face of Augusta, Georgia for all of our partners worldwide. Therefore, if any of our partners have a business referral for Augusta, Micki just became (5) that referral destination. And, unlike the "lead generation" internet sites that have produced a significant number of "experts" who pay to represent certain areas,

(6) The Faces Of only promotes ONE partner per community. For as long as Micki chooses to partner with us, she will be the only Face of Augusta, Georgia. Period.

After her first few days as a partner, Micki sent me a note. It read:

> "Most would define me as resourceful and a real go-getter. I have built a great business over the years with these attributes. Yet, with aging parents, I was forced to relocate and enter into a totally new marketplace with no existing relationships or a book of business. So, when presented with the opportunity to be the host of The Faces of Augusta, Georgia, I was beyond ecstatic and overjoyed, which translated into immediate action for me. I wanted to see how impactful this project could be and the response from the community-at-large. The Faces Of gives a faith-based realtor/broker like me the opportunity to refocus on old-fashion values by reflecting upon a time when you knew your neighbors well. With my first mention of this to my community, I received an overwhelming number of local individuals wanting to participate in the interview process. This system is an Ace of Diamonds. Here's the thing that I have noticed while conducting interviews, it feels like two old friends sitting down for a quick chat. You quickly become familiar with the other and there are no barriers—They immediately open up to you by sharing their story. This tool easily

helps anyone develop a relationship driven business in comparison to being sales driven."

Micki Esposito

Realtor, Momentous Realty

The Faces of Augusta, Georgia

Thank you, Micki Esposito. I hope you have a wonderful time with The Faces of Augusta, Georgia.

What happens when Realtors retire or move away? The majority of them do exactly that: retire or move away. Their business immediately stops. It dries up. Micki's business was in another town, but she has found success in Augusta all the same with assistance from The Faces Of. She will undoubtedly build a fantastic empire in Augusta because she is the host of The Faces of Augusta. This asset in her business will (7) increase the value of her business. One of these days, she will be able to sell her business, or she will be able to bring on junior partners to run it for her. Retired or moved away, the credibility and stability of Micki's business will still carry her through many years in her life after real estate.

And finally, being the host of The Faces of Your Community will not only make you incredibly visible, popular, and relevant, but it will also (8) make you distinctive. You will have differentiated yourself from everyone else in your business.

Do you have to join The Faces Of as a partner to have success? Of course not. But we would love to have you. We will coach and guide each of our partners, including you, along their journey with us no matter what. We hope you are able to join our network.

15

CONCLUSION

I will leave you with some lines from *The Go-Giver*. According to one of the book's characters, Sam, he says, "In any business you need to know how to develop a network. Now, by a network I don't necessarily mean your customers or your clients. I mean a network of people who know you, like you, and trust you. They might never buy a thing from you, but they have always got you in the backs of their minds. They are people who are personally invested in seeing you succeed. And, of course, that is because you are the same way about them. They are your army of personal walking ambassadors. When you have got your own army of personal walking ambassadors, you will have referrals coming your way faster than you can handle them."

Does this describe your network?

Sam went on to say, "The thing that makes this kind of network happen is to stop keeping score. When you base your relationships --in business or anywhere else in your life --on who owes who what, that is not being a friend. That is being a creditor."

The main character, Pindar, asserts, "If you place another person's interests first, your interests will always be taken care of. Always.

Most people would say that money, position, and a history of outstanding accomplishments create influence. Of course that is what most people would say, and they would have it exactly backwards. Those things do not create influence. Influence creates them. And the thing that creates influence is putting other people's interests first."

Looking back and looking forward, I would like to end this story with a few of my observations. Many ideas, business or otherwise, are never implemented. Most never get past the first failure. This has been the story of one that did.

Take time to pause. My real estate group is like a family to me. On top of our office white board is the word PAUSE. We believe we should take time to pause occasionally. We pause to be grateful for our group, for our clients, for our profession, to write notes to people who we want to hear from us, and to give thanks to God for our blessings. I was pushed and encouraged to pause and take some time off from work. I was encouraged to do so by my wife, Jill, by my partner, Regina, and by our office manager, Jennifer. In the beginning, it took letting go. Now, I have paused to share this with you.

Work with discipline. I owe this lesson to my father, J. Bradley Abernathy. He taught me to show up, work harder and smarter, and that anything worth doing is worth doing right.

Collaborate whenever possible. A single right collaboration can have a much higher energy and output than the sum of many working on the same task. Regina and I had twenty-three combined sales the year before we collaborated and forty the year after. Our collaborative group has ranked in the top fifty for sales in our state for the last six years.

Surround yourself with great people. Many have said you can tell a lot about someone by the five to ten people they spend the most time with.

Read and educate yourself. When you find a great idea, concept, or teaching, learn all you can about it and find a way to use it in your life.

Implement. If there is something you want in your life, work hard to make it a reality.

Visualize. Create vision boards for yourself. Put words and pictures on paper to represent you, your life, and the things you want in your life in the future. Use pictures with emotion that show how you will feel when your life is a reflection of your vision board. Many things can be implemented just by focusing on them a few minutes every day.

I am genuinely excited to see what happens with The Faces Of and our partners. From the moment we created the cost effective efficient way to provide The Faces Of to our franchise partners, we added partners in several Georgia communities including Dawsonville and Athens. Most recently, we have added Saint Simons Island and Roswell to the list. Then, we had partners join us in Florida, Alabama, and Tennessee. Remember a real estate coach named Clara Capano? She was the one who taught me the Ninja System. She loved The Faces Of and helped us add partners in several other communities, some located as far as Colorado. Others along the way have shared The Faces Of with people they know, which helped us add partners in New York, California, Mississippi, Pennsylvania, Wisconsin, Illinois, Ohio, Washington, Texas, and North Carolina. As I write this book, we are in several conversations with business men and women from Michigan, Minnesota, Hawaii, and Canada. Like Brian Weiss said, "We are building a celebration of community from coast to coast."

The future of this platform will be an international brand for The Faces Of. As it grows, each of our community partners will benefit greatly from support, from idea sharing among partners, from the name brand's growth and recognition, from being connected to community influencers around the world, and from the referral business connections this will provide.

I will commit to my partners the following: We will provide value to you and a plan. You will be given the tools to do for your community exactly what we have done for our community. If you will allow us to coach you, we will do so. If you follow our plan, you will rise in visibility, relevance, and influence in your community. You will be quickly known as a master at marketing in your community, and you will soon have an army of supporters who want to see you succeed. You will not be spending thousands of dollars buying leads. You will be creating real relationships and becoming the ambassador of your community. You will become a leader in your community in no time.

The Faces Of, LLC is owned and operated by The Abernathy Cochran Group, LLC, located at 434 Green Street, Gainesville, Georgia, 30501. Our business partner is Veugeler Design Group, LLC, located at 554 West Main Street, Suite 200, Buford, Georgia, 30518. The Faces Of, LLC, has copyright protections and has been issued service mark protections in the United States of America. For more information, please contact us anytime. Visit us online at www.thefacesof.com or email brad@thefacesof.com.

ACKNOWLEDGEMENT

I said not long ago you can tell a lot about someone by the five to ten people with whom they spend most of their time. These are ten who have made my life rich.

I thank my wife, **Jill Venable Abernathy**, for an amazing twenty-three years of marriage. She is a true friend to so many and a counselor to many others, including to me. She tells the truth. If this book ever gets published, it is because she finally gave me the okay, or I did not let her read it first. She is unique like a snowflake, yet fragile like a bomb. She is the best mother my children could have ever hoped for. Our children love to spend time with us, which is one of her huge successes. Thank you, Jill, for being everything to our family. You, Sadie, and Kate are my favorite people in the whole world.

John Canupp is the best friend anyone could wish for. He has supported me since we were fifteen. I love him like a brother. He is an educator now and is preparing to be Realtor with me in the second phase of his career. I honestly can not wait to spend more time with him. I am very grateful that John invited me on that first golf trip. We just got home from our fourth such trip where we spent a week on Amelia Island, Florida.

Robert Bell is one of the smartest and funniest people you could ever meet. The first time I ever dreamed of collaborating with anyone it was going to be with Robert. I could call Robert at 3AM if I needed him, and he would be there 100% of the time.

Chris Romberg has introduced me to the three C's: canoeing, civic leadership responsibilities, and craft beer. We were neighbors, then great friends, and now he has joined our group as a Realtor. He would give me the shirt of his back if I needed it. He has been there for me in the hardest times of my life.

Jennifer Skogman is one of the smartest people I know. I love how her mind works. If people think it is hard to read me, and I have heard that for all of my life, good luck reading Jennifer. She will not only tell you what she thinks, she will stare you down first. She thinks before she speaks, and she holds back nothing. I knew I was taking a risk when I let her read the first draft of this book before anyone else saw it. For a full two days, I waited and braced myself for her feedback.

People in my business and those that do business with our group all say they need a **Rosemary Hancock**. Rosemary is our office manager, and she is the second newest person on this list in my life. She is also the only millennial. Rosemary's support and desire to stick with me "forever" – her words – mean a great deal. When she is out of the office she says, "Don't let anyone sit in this chair. This is my desk."

Many said early on that my business partnership with **Regina Cochran** was something unexpected. I was struggling financially during the Great Recession. She had no hair as she was undergoing chemotherapy treatment for a second time in her life. Amid treatments and with a scarf tied around her head, I watched this amazing woman outwork every other Realtor in our company during the recession. I believe God brought us together. My life is so much better today and every day since she agreed to be my business partner. She is one of the strongest people I know.

Personal notes from **Frank Norton, Jr.** started showing up in my mailbox over a decade ago. Frank wanted to meet with me. He wanted me to come work with him at the Norton Agency. Frank has been a great supporter and mentor of mine. He was there for me when my father died. He was there for Regina and I when we wanted to try something new and it worked. Frank is an amazingly creative person. He loves to help others succeed.

I felt that God blessed The Faces Of business early on. This was evident when we partnered with Angie Veugeler's company. It became more evident when I met **Brian Weiss**. Brian is an influencer and an energizer. He will help this company grow from one location to fifty states and several countries. The similarities between Brian and I are a little uncanny. I believe we will add value to thousands of people's lives together and celebrate relationships and communities across the world. We will be friends and business partners for a long time.

My father, **Bradley Abernathy,** taught me many things. May he rest in peace. I will never forget him. Unfortunately, though many of the things he taught me lead to my life now, he left us too early to see them become reality. His father left his family much too early as well. His father, Papa Ford, died at forty. My father died at sixty-eight. Some see those numbers and think the average of them is fifty-four. All of these people above have contributed to my life and my positive outlook. So, when I see those numbers I see the interval. The next number would be ninety-six.

Last month, May 2019, I turned forty-eight. I suppose that makes me exactly middle aged. The next forty-eight years are going to be unbelievably amazing. I love my life, my family, and my career. I love the people who surround me and make me better. I love the people in my community who I get to meet each week. And I am very grateful to each of you who made it to the end of my first book.

WORKS CITED

Burg, Bob and Mann, John David. "The Five Laws of Stratospheric Success." *The Go-Giver*, Portfolio / Penguin, Penquin Random House, LLC., 2015, New York, New York

Burg, Bob and Mann, John David. "The Law of Influence." *The Go-Giver*, Portfolio / Penguin, Penquin Random House, LLC., 2015, New York, New York

Kendall, Larry. "The Power of 8 in 8." *Ninja Selling*, Greenleaf Book Group Press, 2017, Austin, Texas